Terry Treble and Letter H W...

A Terry Treble Music Ad...

Book I

Published by
MusicLearningCommunity.com, LLC

Illustrated by
Genevieve Bergeson

Terry Treble and Letter H Write Music:
A Terry Treble Music Adventure
Book I

Copyright © 2013 MusicLearningCommunity.com, LLC

Published by MusicLearningCommunity.com, LLC
Written by Bill Hermanson
Illustrated by Genevieve Bergeson

ISBN: 978-0-9910294-0-2

Are you ready to come play music?

All musicians know that the notes of the music staff are A, B, C, D, E, F, and G. But not everyone knows that there used to be an H note, too. This is the story of the beginning of written music and why we don't see an H note today.

Centuries ago, when people started playing music, they wanted to find a way to save music so it it could be played more than once. With no way to keep music, it just disappeared after it was played. That was sad, because some music was very beautiful, and people wanted to hear it again and again.

Back in those days, record players, iPods, radio, and television had not been invented yet, so you couldn't just listen to a recording. Musicians had to remember what they played if they wanted to play the same music over and over again. But when a musician went away, no one could enjoy the music until the musician came back (unless someone else had learned it).

Terry Treble decided to do something about this problem.

Terry Treble was smart, and he knew the alphabet and how to read books. He also loved to hear and sing music. So Terry thought and thought about how to keep music. And then he got a brilliant idea! Ideas are kept and given to others by writing them down in books. Why not *write* music, too?

But there was another problem! Music is sound. How do you write sound?

Some of Terry Treble's friends, the letters and numbers, came to play, and he told them what he was trying to do. His good friend Letter H had an idea.

"When letters are put together in a book to make a word, and you say the word, it becomes sound. That is like sound on paper."

There was the answer! Terry Treble had to put letters on paper to make sound words.

Terry Treble decided to try some singing experiments with his friends. Terry asked Letter A, Letter J, and Letter F to line up, and he gave each of them a sound to sing when he pointed at them. So they did. And it was awful! It was not music at all. It was just sound. Terry Treble thought that maybe those friends were not doing it right, so he tried again with Letter C, Letter D, and Letter E. It was a little better, but still it was only sound, not music!

Terry Treble could not figure out exactly what was wrong. But he was determined to find a way to save music on paper like words in books.

"I won't give up," Terry said. "Since letters on paper keep ideas as words, there must be a way to keep music on paper, too. I just need to think some more to find the answer."

When Terry Treble needed to think, he liked to go to the pond in the woods. It was always beautiful and peaceful. Some insects were buzzing around, and a gentle breeze blew. It was so quiet, warm, and peaceful that Terry Treble fell asleep.

Some birds flew overhead and landed in the trees. Then they began to sing. Terry woke up and heard them. Their beautiful sound made him more determined to figure out how to keep music.

The birds quieted down a little. Terry Treble noticed that five songbirds sat on different branches above each other. One bird sang. Then another. And another.

"Wow," thought Terry. "That's it!" When his friends sang, they sang all at once, and it was sound, but not music. When all the birds sang at the same time, sometimes it was like music, and sometimes it was noisy. But when they sang different sounds one after the other, it sounded a lot more like music.

Terry Treble ran back to the playground where his friends still were. Excitedly he told them what the birds' singing had suggested—that they should not all sing at once, but one at a time. So Terry lined up Letters A, J, F, and B. Then Terry pointed to each one—one at a time—and each letter sang a sound. This time the result was much better! It was not quite music yet, but Terry Treble knew that this was progress.

What else was needed to save music on paper? When you read a book, no one points at the words—you just read them one after another. How do you make a bunch of letters that are sounds turn into music?

Just then, Letter H came up to talk with Terry about the problem. Remember, Letter H had suggested that words on paper could be sounds. While they were talking, Terry Treble remembered something about the birds in the trees. They had sat on different branches and made different sounds. The bird on the lowest branch sang one sound, and the one on the branch above it sang another sound. This gave Terry another idea.

Terry Treble found five sticks and placed them on the ground, one above the other. Next, he asked Letters A, J, F, B, and H to each stand on a different stick. Each letter was given a sound to sing.

Then Terry Treble stood at one end of the sticks and—this is the special thing—told them, "Sing only one sound, after the letter on the branch next to you sings."

So they did. And Terry Treble smiled. And Letter H smiled. And Letter J, Letter A, Letter B, and Letter F smiled. This was music! Well, almost music. It still was not quite right, but it sounded very, very good.

"Okay," said Terry, "what have we learned so far about keeping music?"

Letter H spoke up right away. "We should sing one at a time, not all at once."

Letter J said, "Letters have to have different sounds, like the birds."

Letter B asked, "Sometimes we hear more than one music sound at the same time and it sounds good. Why is that?" No one had an answer for that just yet.

Then Number 8 said, "Words are organized. When you put certain letters together, you get certain words. Different combinations make different words."

All the letters except H started playing at making different words. As Terry and Letter H watched them, Letter H said, "Number 8 may have the right idea: organized letters make words. And letters are organized in the alphabet. We could put the letters in alphabetical order."

"That's a good idea," Terry said. "Let's try it."

So Terry Treble and Letter H called to some of the other letters to come back. Letters C, E, J, and G came, but the others kept playing. Terry Treble put Letter C, Letter E, and Letter G on the first three branches in the sand. Then Terry Treble put Letter H on the fourth one and Letter J on the fifth one (C E G H J).

"Now," said Terry Treble, "we will start with Letter C on the first branch. Letter C will sing a 'knot'—that is what we will call a single sound, just like the knots in the tree branches. Then, in order, the rest of you will sing a knot that is a little different from the others. Since Letter C is on the lowest branch, Letter E needs to sing a knot just a little higher, and Letter G a knot just a little higher than that." Then Terry Treble stood at the end of the branches and said "Start."

So Letter C sang, then Letter E sang, then Letter G, then Letter H, and finally Letter J. They were making music!

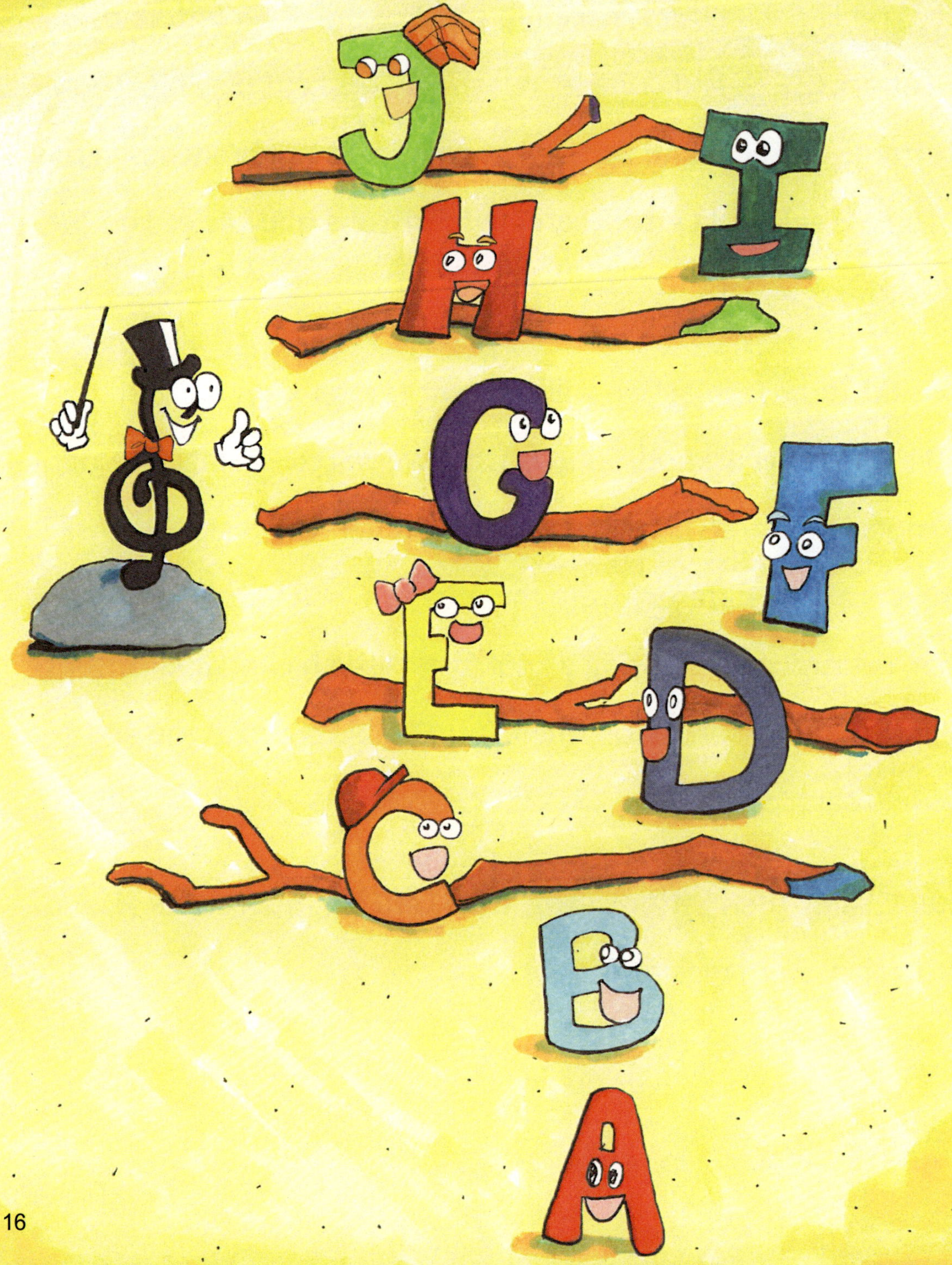
J
I
H
G
F
E
D
C
B
A

Some of the other letters came over to be part of the music. To keep the letters in alphabetical order, Terry Treble put Letter D in the space between Letter C and Letter E, put Letter F between E and G, and put Letter I between H and J. Letter A and Letter B complained that they were being left out, so Terry put them in order below Letter C, even though there were no more branches to stand on.

Terry Treble explained what they were doing again and started with Letter C once more. He also told Letter A and Letter B to sing knots that were steps lower than Letter C's knot. Then Terry Treble stood at the end of the branches and said "Start." Letter A sang, then Letter B, then Letter C, then Letter D, all the way up to Letter I. And it was really fun. It was music!

"Okay," said Terry Treble, "we have the idea now! I think we have solved the main problem. We need to have letters sing individual knots and then organize the letters the right way to be music. Now if we adjust a bit, maybe we will have a way to save music on paper." Terry Treble did not know right then that there was a lot more to music than what had been learned so far, but learning about it was a lot of fun, and the rest would be learned at the right time.

All of them had had so much fun figuring out how to keep music that they did not realize how late it was getting. As everyone went home for the night, each letter sang the knot he or she had learned to memorize it for tomorrow.

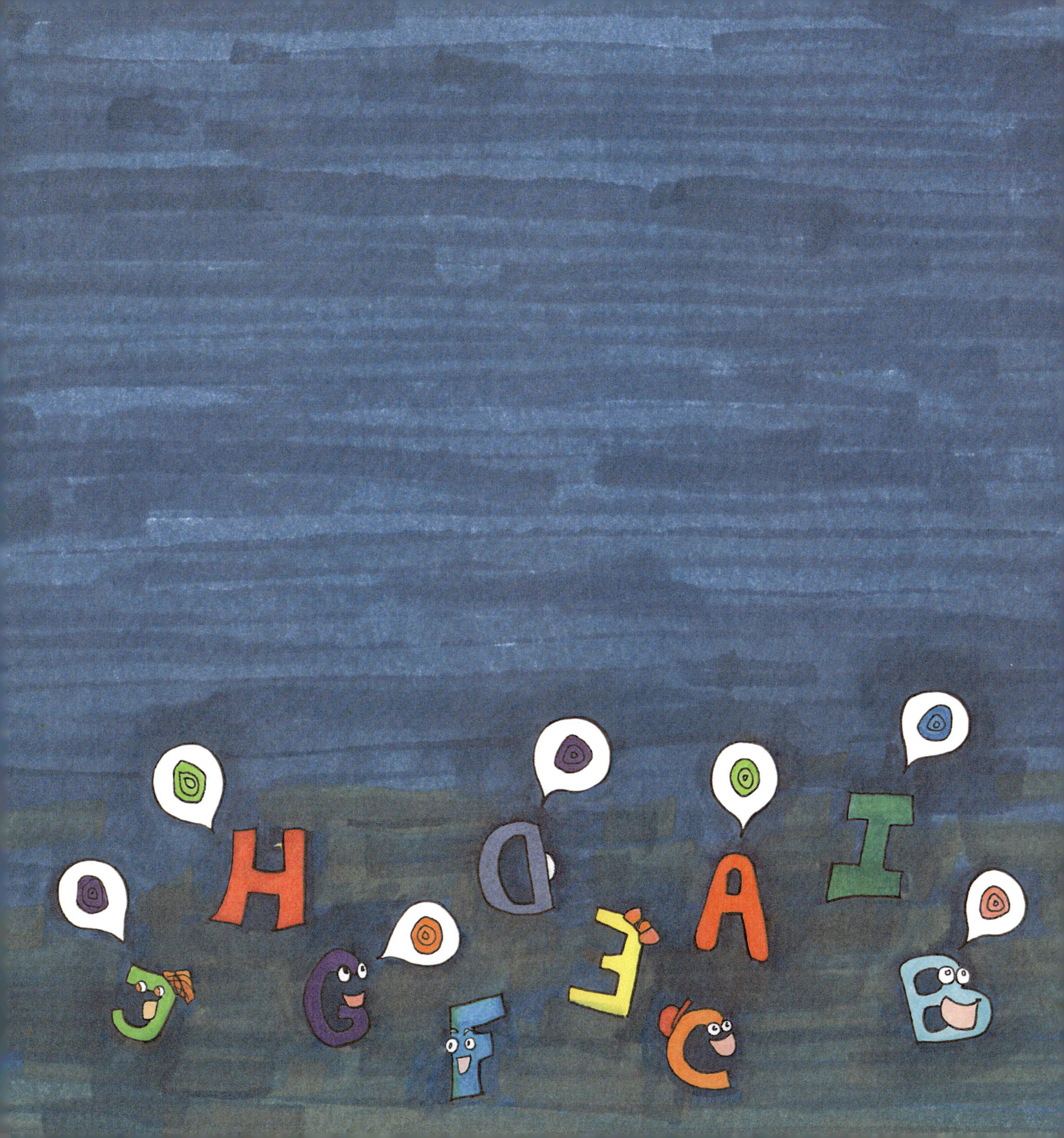

The next day, Terry Treble was excited to get started on the music project again. As soon as breakfast was finished, he raced to the playground. Letter E, Letter G, and Letter H were already there, so Terry asked them to stand on the first three branches and practice their knots. Soon Letter C and Letter D came, and they took their positions in alphabetical order. This time, they were below the first branch. When Letter J came later, he stood above Letter H (C D E F G H J).

Since they were standing on different sticks than yesterday, they had to learn new knots. Soon they learned to sing a step or two above or below the others and were making music again.

The knot was related to the stick. If you stood on one stick, you sang one knot, and on another stick another knot.

Letter H and Letter J decided to do something else for a while, so they went to the other side of the playground to play. When Letter A and Letter B came a few minutes later to do more music, Terry Treble put them in place of Letter H and Letter J. But when they started singing, they sang the knots they had learned yesterday! That did not work because they were standing on different sticks than yesterday. But soon they also learned new knots, and the singing sounded good again.

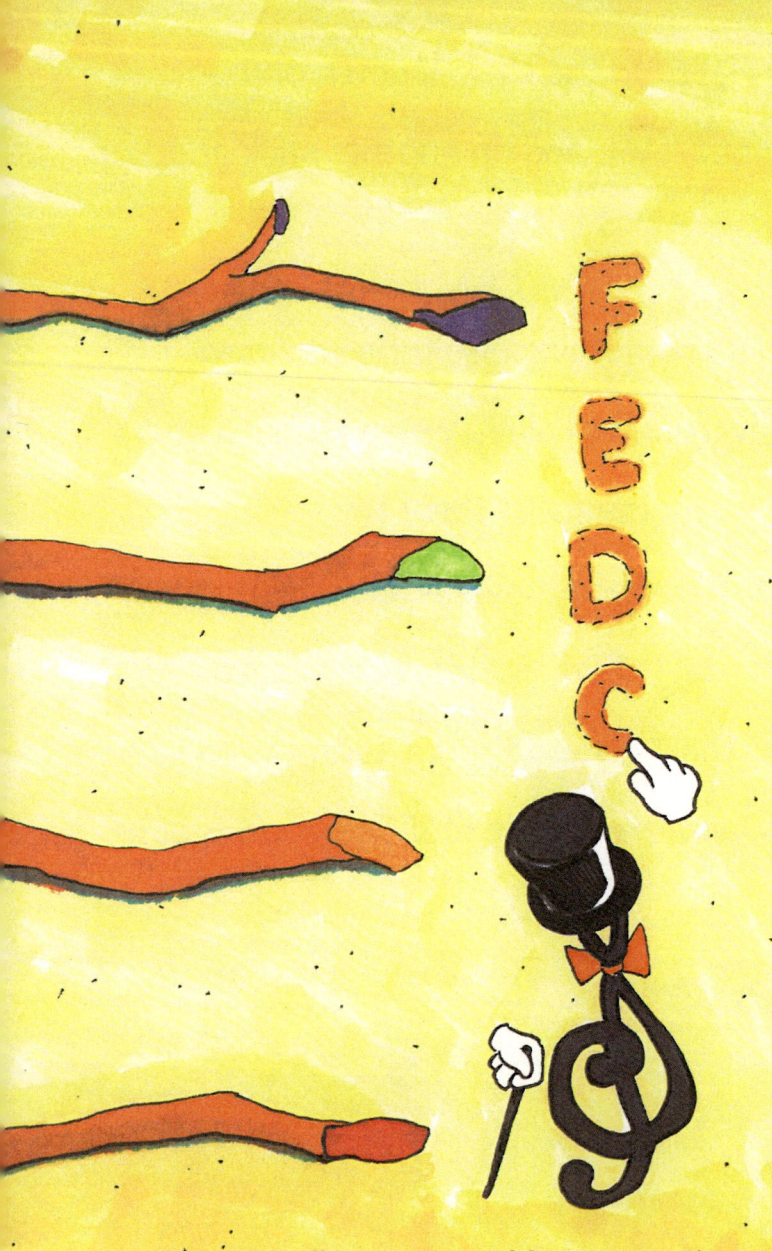

Terry Treble thought about this for a moment. It took time for the letters to keep learning new knots. Maybe they should learn just one knot really well and always sing the same knot. But the letters had to learn new knots because they stood on different sticks.

So the letters should always stand on the same sticks!

Terry Treble suggested that they label the sticks so that in the future they would not waste time trying to figure out who was to sing which knot. So, he wrote in the sand next to each stick "E", "G", "B", "D", and "F". That meant that the spaces between the sticks were "F", "A", "C", and "E".

When Terry stepped back to look, they realized that they had used the letter "E" twice—once for the bottom stick and once for the top space. They had used "F" twice, too—once for the first space and once for the top stick. They also saw that the space just below the first stick was "D" and that the fourth stick was also "D". This was very, very interesting; every eighth letter was the same. So the same letter had to know two knots seven notes apart—seven steps up or seven steps down.

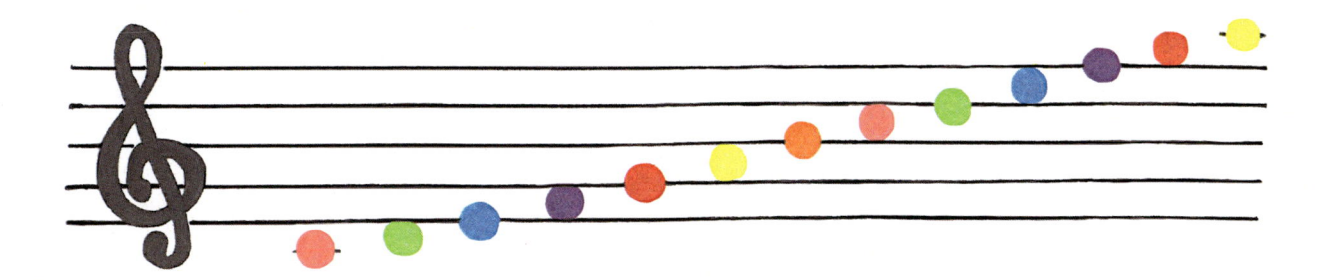

So what they did with sticks in the sand they could do on paper to keep music. Terry Treble drew five lines on a page of his notebook and marked each line with a letter (E G B D F). Each line and space would always have its own same note to sing.

To make a long story a little shorter, you all know that today the music staff has five lines in place of the five sticks, and the lines are labeled "E", "G", "B", "D", and "F". And because Letter H and Letter J went off to play, line B is B instead of H, and today there is no H note, just the notes (not knots) in groups of eight, "C, D, E, F, G, A, B, C." And those five lines and spaces are called the "staff," and the "treble clef" stands at the beginning of it.

Terry Treble and Letter H had discovered the first part of how to put music on paper with musical notation so that music that someone composed could be saved. Someone else who had never heard the music before could play it just like the original. Isn't that really, really wonderful!

But we are not done with the story of Letter H. When Letter H came back from playing with Letter J and found out that the stick was labeled "B" instead of "H", Letter H felt a little sad. There was no place for Letter H to stand anymore. But Terry Treble and Letter H were really good friends, so Terry Treble made a suggestion.

"You know," he said, "I noticed that when I listen to music, there are a lot more knots than those on my sticks. I think we should have another set of sticks for those knots. You could take care of that and name them yourself."

Have you ever heard of the "bass clef"? Well, that is another story.

Author's Comments

There really was (is) an H note, although not as originated in this Terry Treble fiction. In German musical nomenclature, the note B natural is written as H and B flat as B.

A common *motif*, or series of notes that are important or characteristic to a musical work, is the BACH motif, named after the German Baroque composer Johann Sebastian Bach (1685-1750). He frequently incorporated those notes in that order into his compositions. More recent composers have used the motif, too, most often to give homage to Bach.

B is one of the seven standard notes in the *diatonic scale.* "Diatonic" comes from a Greek word meaning "progressing through tones." Starting with C, the notes are C, D, E, F, G, A, and B. The seven notes are arranged along a certain pattern of *half steps* and *whole steps* (whole, whole, half, whole, whole, whole, whole, half). All the half steps are separated from each other by at least two whole steps. Starting on a different note than C makes other notes in the scale higher or lower than their normal pitches. The higher ones are called *sharps,* and the lower ones are called *flats.*

Sharps are marked by this symbol: ♯

Flats are marked by this symbol: ♭

The seven diatonic pitches are just a small subset of the notes in use in tuning systems and scales around the world. The modern Western convention uses twelve tones. This tuning system was created to do multiple things:

1. Use fifth-based intervals from the historic diatonic scale

2. Use the full *chromatic scale* (which incorporates all the half steps between the standard diatonic notes)

3. Let the musician move easily between musical keys.

Middle Eastern and Indian music use finer subdivisions of the octave, for example, in the Arabic twenty-four tone scale. Also, most cultures use expressive *microtones* that fall between the "official" scale notes. You hear microtones all the time in blues and its descendants—rock, jazz, country, etc.

The oldest known form of written music is on a cuneiform tablet made in Iraq around 2000 B.C. and was written based on a diatonic scale. (Cuneiform is an ancient form of writing.)

If you would like to order another copy of this or other Terry Treble books, please visit the website TerryTreble.com or MusicLearningCommmunity.com